lonely planet

NOT-FOR-PARENTS

ASIA
Everything
you ever
wanted
to know

Margaret Hyn

D1332953

C015717298

CONTENTS

THAT'S A BIG WORD. SHALL I ASK SIR?

I WONDER WHAT THIS IS?

LOOKS LIKE IT NEEDS CHOCOLATE ON IT.

OK, LET'S START OFF WITH A NICE CUP OF TEA!

NOT-FOR-PARENTS

THIS IS NOT A GUIDEBOOK. And it is definitely Not-for-Parents.

IT IS THE REAL INSIDE STORY about one of the world's most exciting continents – Asia. In this book you'll hear fascinating tales about **Samurai warriors** and Bollywood legends, fabulous carpets, explosive volcanoes and **modern-day pirates**.

Check out cool stories about hunting with **golden eagles**, dog astronauts, guerilla warfare and eccentric dictators. You'll find holy cows, **purple people**, some seriously tough mountain folk and **history** galore.

This book shows you an **ASIA** your parents probably don't even know about.

FROZEN OUT

If you don't like crowds, the countryside in northern Russia is the place for you. On average, there is just one person for every square kilometre (247 acres) there. This is hardly surprising – temperatures in winter can plummet to –60°C (–76°F), freezing the ground solid for months at a time.

Kazakhstan

Uzbekistan

Kyrgyzstan

Turkmenistan

Tajikistan

Syria

Lebanon

Afghanistan

Israel **Jordan**

Iraq

Iran

Kuwait

Pakistan

Nep

Qatar

Saudi Arabia **U.A.E.**

India

Oman

Mega Mecca

The usual population of Mecca in Saudi Arabia is 2 million people. This number more than triples each year during the Hajj, when Muslims from all over the world make a pilgrimage to religious sites in the city.

Yemen

Sri Lanka

BUSY ASIA

Asia covers a third of the planet, yet it is home to 60 per cent of the world's population. It is very crowded in some places. On average each square kilometre (247 acres) of Manila (the Philippines' capital), is home to 43,000 people. And in the slums there are twice as many people. On the other hand, hardly anyone lives in deepest northern Russia.

Russia

Mongolia

China

North Korea

South Korea

Japan

Bhutan

Bangladesh

Myanmar Laos

Thailand

Vietnam

Cambodia

Philippines

Taiwan

M a l a y s i a

Brunei

I n d o n e s i a

Timor-Leste

WHO'S THE DADDY?

Genghis Khan is! One in every 12 Asians living today is a descendant of the fearsome Mongolian warrior. So, this means that since the 13th century, the Khan family has grown to 32 million people. Try drawing that family tree!

NO KIDDING!

In 1978, the Chinese government declared that families could have only one child because the country was getting too crowded. The plan slowed down population growth, but it is still high, with 50,000 babies being born each day – that's about 35 every minute!

WANT MORE?

DESERT DINOSAURS

In the early 1920s, a US expedition led by Roy Chapman Andrews unearthed a treasure trove of dinosaur fossils from the Cretaceous Period (165–66 million years ago). The Gobi Desert, which covers large parts of China and Mongolia, has been a major hunting ground for fossil-seekers ever since.

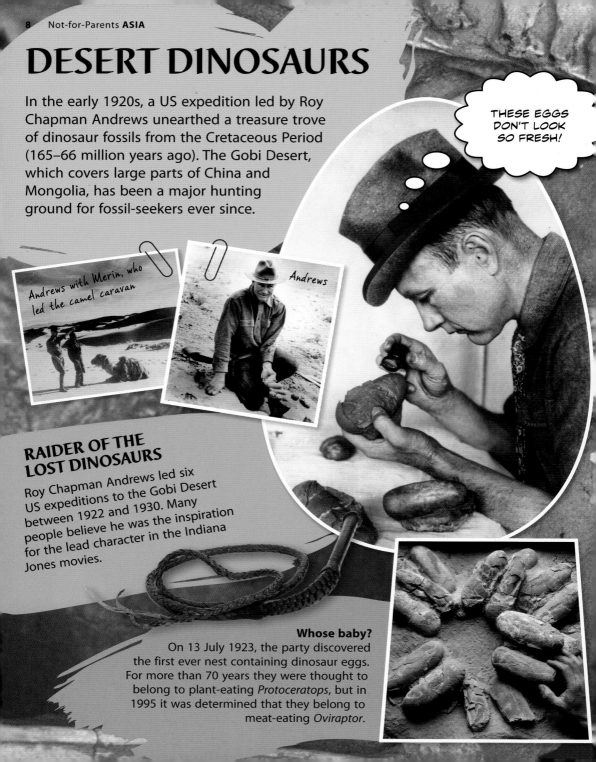

Andrews with Merin, who led the camel caravan

Andrews

THESE EGGS DON'T LOOK SO FRESH!

RAIDER OF THE LOST DINOSAURS

Roy Chapman Andrews led six US expeditions to the Gobi Desert between 1922 and 1930. Many people believe he was the inspiration for the lead character in the Indiana Jones movies.

Whose baby?

On 13 July 1923, the party discovered the first ever nest containing dinosaur eggs. For more than 70 years they were thought to belong to plant-eating *Protoceratops*, but in 1995 it was determined that they belong to meat-eating *Oviraptor*.

Fossil hunters' trucks in the Gobi Desert

FOSSIL FINDS

1923 - Velociraptor, Psittacosaurus, Protoceratops and Oviraptor, including Oviraptor eggs

1971 - Juvenile Velociraptor attacking a Protoceratops

2011 - Nest of 15 young Protoceratops

Sands of time

The sandy and rocky terrain of the Gobi Desert is a difficult place to search for fossils. But it was different when the dinosaurs lived there in the Cretaceous Period. Then, the rich and fertile landscape was criss-crossed by rivers and dotted with lakes.

Fossil of Velociraptor vs Protoceratops

Sandy slog

Members of the expeditions often had to push their vehicles through the sand.

Caring parents

In 2011, a nest of 15 young *Protoceratops* was discovered in Mongolia. The discovery suggests that *Protoceratops* parents cared for their young in nests during at least the early stages of infancy.

Deadly embrace

In 1971, a fossil of *Velociraptor* and *Protoceratops* locked in combat was discovered in the desert. The dinosaurs were buried alive 80 million years ago, during a landslide. The *Velociraptor* had grasped its victim's head in its front claws and dug its back feet into its belly.

LOOK, DAD'S COME TO CHECK ON US.

WANT MORE?

Dino pit ✶ http://kids.nationalgeographic.co.uk/kids/stories/spacescience/dino-death-pit/

TUNNEL RATS

Conventional warfare techniques weren't effective in the tunnel war, so the US Army was forced to adopt basic hand-to-hand combat. Small volunteers were trained to become tunnel specialists, known as 'rats'. Usually stripped to the waist and armed with just a torch and a pistol, the rats would spend hours at a time inching through the tunnels in a deadly game of hide-and-seek.

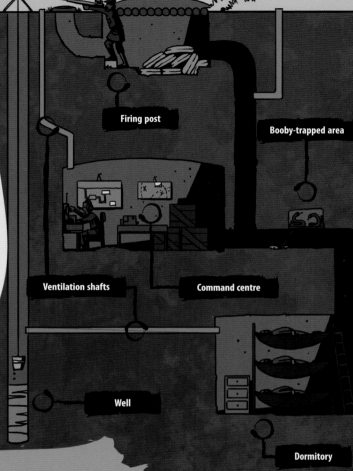

Firing post

Booby-trapped area

Ventilation shafts

Command centre

Well

Dormitory

UNDERGROUND MOVEMENT

During the 1960s and 1970s, Vietnamese soldiers called the Viet Cong fought a guerilla war against American forces from underground tunnels. The cleverly hidden tunnel system stretched across Vietnam. Life underground was harsh. The spaces were humid and cramped, the air was poor, and there were lots of insects and rats.

The underworld
The tunnels weren't just narrow passages. Some tunnels contained kitchens, dormitories, command centres, hospitals and theatres. Ventilation shafts helped to keep the temperature down, and were useful for hearing enemy helicopters.

Kitchen

The Viet Cong ate, slept and fought in the tunnels.

In some areas the tunnels have been widened so that visiting Western tourists can fit through them.

WATCH OUT. IT MIGHT BE TRAPPED!

Booby-trapped area

Booby-trapped area

Rat traps
The tunnels were filled with a range of deadly booby traps. Boxes of scorpions, or highly venomous snakes, were carefully placed to tip over any unsuspecting intruders. In other areas, Viet Cong soldiers waited to ambush unwelcome visitors, or a trapdoor in the floor hid a pit of razor-sharp stakes. The tunnels were also built with bends to stop the enemy from shooting through them in a straight line.

The Viet Cong, or National Liberation Front, helped North Vietnam defeat the South Vietnamese government and their American allies in the Vietnam War (1959–75).

Storage room

WANT MORE?

Key Vietnam dates ★ www.history.com/topics/vietnam-war

ALL ABOARD

Armed only with a pair of white gloves and a flag, Tokyo's *oshiya*, or pushers, have been keeping the city's rail network moving since the early 1930s. They manage this by literally squashing as many people as possible into already overcrowded carriages during the morning and evening rush hours.

PUSHY PEOPLE

Just before the train departs, the oshiyas ram passengers into carriages. Then they signal for the doors to be closed, before checking that no bags, or even passengers, are stuck in them. Trapped passengers are either pushed in, or pulled out!

YEY! A WINDOW SPACE, NOT A SMELLY ARMPIT!

4 million
commuters travel into Tokyo each day.

Crush hour comforts
Rush hour is an uncomfortable affair. The packed trains are hot and claustrophobic. There is certainly no room to stretch, and most people are crammed into spaces where they can barely move.

PASSENGER POWER

Japan is a high-tech nation, so it's hardly surprising that it has found a way of harnessing the energy created by its capital's many commuters. Electricity-generating pads are embedded into the floor in some stations. The pads are connected to digital displays, which let the commuters know how much energy their footwork is creating.

Good to go
After the doors are safely closed, the oshiya lifts up a flag, to signal to the conductor or driver that it is safe to go.

WANT MORE?

Pushers ☆ www.kawaiikakkoiisugoi.com/2011/06/14/tokyo-subway-packers-push-people-around/

PURPLE PEOPLE

The Phoenicians were the greatest traders of their time (1500–300 BC). They controlled a narrow coastal strip in the area of present-day Lebanon. Their name comes from the Greek *phoinikois*, referring to the purple dye that helped make them so successful. Their major cities were Arwad, Byblos, Sidon and Tyre – where the finest purple dye was produced.

Phoenician ports were busy trading centres.

I WONDER WHO'S GOING TO WEAR THIS – A KING, AN EMPEROR...

HEY, BIG SPENDER

Although other people made purple dye, none made it as well as the Phoenicians. Tyrian purple, in particular, was highly sought after because it was vibrant and didn't fade. This meant that Phoenician traders could demand big bucks for their dyed textiles.

Murex shells

Fashion victims

The purple dye was made using two sea snails – the spiny *Murex trunculus* and the smaller *Baccinum lapillus*. A gooey mucus was extracted from the *Murex*, while the *Baccinum* was crushed whole. The pulp was then mixed with salt, and left to simmer in a heated cauldron for almost two weeks. Cloth was dipped in the dye to get the famous violet-purple.

DIED FOR THE RICH

Since more than 10,000 sea snails were needed to dye a single garment, the colour was very costly to make and buy. It was so highly prized that it became a status symbol, worn by emperors, kings and important religious people.

Big stink
The leftover bits of the Murex were tossed into piles and left to rot. This created something of a stink. In fact, it was so smelly that visitors tended to avoid the coast during the hot summer months. They just didn't have the nose for it.

Each Murex gave a single drop of yellow mucus that turned purple when exposed to light.

Basket bait
Baccinum are found stuck to rocks in shallow water, so they could be picked by hand. But *Murex* live in deeper water, and had to be caught in baskets baited with frogs or mussels!

WHY ME? I DON'T EVEN LIKE PURPLE!

WANT MORE?

Phoenicians ★ www.kidspast.com/world-history/0044-phoenicians.php

MORE THAN JUST TEA

In Japan, making a cup of tea can be a very special event. The Japanese tea-making ceremony is a spiritual experience, strongly influenced by Zen Buddhism. The history of the ceremony goes back more than 1000 years, when the first tea leaves were brought back from China by Japanese priests. The ceremony can last up to four hours, and sometimes includes a three-course meal.

The powdered *maccha* tea leaves are kept in a lidded pot called a *chaki*.

HAVE YOU EVER CONSIDERED TEABAGS?

Tea-whisks, used to mix the tea and water, are carved from a single piece of bamboo.

Many people take tea ceremony lessons, though becoming a tea master can take many years.

PUT THE KETTLE ON

During the tea ceremony, a charcoal fire is burnt to heat the metal kettle, which is called a *chagama*.

KNOWING ALL THE ANGLES

The highly ritualized ceremony is steeped in tradition. Each step of the preparation has fixed movements. Utensils and vessels have to be placed at precisely the correct angle in relation to each other and the guests. Everything is carefully done to show grace, tranquillity and respect.

The green tea, made of powdered leaves, is called maccha.

Chawan is the name given to the tea bowl from which the tea is drunk.

Hishaku are used to transfer hot water from the iron kettle to the *chawan*.

WANT MORE?

Tea ceremony ☆ www.japanese-tea-ceremony.net

SURVIVAL OF THE FITTEST

Gurkhas have been part of the British Army for nearly 200 years, but becoming one isn't easy. Every year, tens of thousands of young Nepalese men apply to become new recruits. But there are only 186 places, and the selection process is gruelling. It begins with regional trials, where the numbers are whittled down to 700. These lucky hopefuls are invited to Central Selection in Pokhara, where only the fittest and toughest make the grade.

Recruits must be between 17 and 22, and at least 1.6m (5ft 2in) tall.

UH! MY BACK IS KILLING ME.

CHANCES ARE NUMBERED

During Regional Selection, the candidates have numbers painted on their chest in a special ink that doesn't come off for a few days. This stops them from retrying elsewhere if unsuccessful.

Put through their paces
Successful recruits are invited to the Gurkha camp in Pokhara for Central Selection. Some of the boys travel several days, often on foot, to get there. For the next two weeks they study hard for their selection exams.

Fighting fit?
British Army doctors examine candidates at Central Selection. For many, this is the first time they will have been examined by a doctor, and the tests often detect serious complaints that had previously gone undiagnosed.

HEAVY-GOING

The Doko Race is the most gruelling part of Central Selection. The men race uphill, carrying 35kg (77lb) of stones in a *doko* basket on their back. This is tougher than any other selection test in the British Army.

CENTRAL SELECTION EXAMS

- Run 2.5km in not more than 9 minutes and 40 seconds
- Complete a 3.2km-uphill route (1.9mi) carrying 35kg (77lb) in less than 48 minutes
- Swimming assessment – complete 20m (22yds)
- Medical tests
- Tests equivalent to GCSE English and Maths

Fond farewell
Before the recruits leave for the UK, their families perform a moving farewell ceremony, hanging flower garlands around the men's necks and daubing their faces with rice and paint.

HMMMM! MAYBE THIS IS A HAYFEVER TEST?!

WANT MORE?

National Army Museum ☆ www.nam.ac.uk/exhibitions/online-exhibitions/gurkhas

COMIC BOOK HEROES

In Japan, it isn't just kids who read comics. They are popular with people of all ages, and millions of Japanese yen are spent on them every year. Japan has a highly destinctive comic style, known as *manga*. Sometimes manga cartoons are made into films, and sometimes films are made into comics.

HONEY, I'M HOME!

MANGA STYLE

While each artist has his or her own style, manga has a distinctive look. The drawings are usually done in pen and ink, and most characters have large, almond-shaped eyes and other out-of-proportion body parts.

He needs some manga management

In many stories, the characters display over-the-top emotions. The artists use special techniques, as well as the characters' eyes and mouths, to depict emotions.

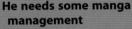

Lines radiating from his body and a clenched fist show this man is full of rage.

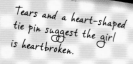

Tears and a heart-shaped tie pin suggest the girl is heartbroken.

Where d'ya get those peepers?
Often considered the Walt Disney of manga, Osamu Tezuka was the first manga illustrator to draw the distinctive large eyes. Tezuka is also the inventor of one of the best-known manga characters, Astro Boy.

COMICONS

Fan conventions, or cons, draw admirers of manga together to meet illustrators, famous personalities and each other. Fans often dress up like their favourite manga characters, or characters of their own creation.

PLEASE CAN I COLOUR IT IN NOW?

THE THREE-TRILLION YEN INDUSTRY

Manga earns three trillion yen (£19.2 billion) a year, and since the year 2000 the Japanese government has recognized it as an official art form. Japanese universities even offer students the opportunity to study manga.

KNOW YOUR MANGA

There are different types of manga:
1. **Shônen** (pronounced Show-Nen) is usually action-packed and humorous.
2. **Shôjo** (pronounced Show-Joe) is light-hearted and romantic.
3. **Josei** or **redikomi** (pronounced Joe-Say) contains romance and super-heroines.
4. **Kodomo** (pronounced Kow-Dow-Mow) is aimed at children, teaching them how to behave as good and considerate people.

WANT MORE?

Men are encouraged to complete the first three of the seven circuits of the Ka'ba quickly.

Tawaf

The Tawaf is one of the rituals of the pilgrimage. The pilgrims walk around the Ka'ba seven times in an anticlockwise direction. Each circuit is started at the Black Stone (set in the wall of the Ka'ba), which pilgrims are expected to kiss. If that's not possible because of the crowds, pilgrims may point towards the stone with their right hand.

PRAISE BE TO ALLAH.

IT'S A MECCA FOR MUSLIMS

Every year, about three million Muslims gather in Mecca in Saudi Arabia, to show their unity and devotion to Allah. All able-bodied Muslims are expected to make this holy journey, called the Hajj, at least once in their lifetime if they can afford it. During the Hajj, pilgrims perform acts of worship before the Ka'ba, a cuboid building that is the most sacred site in Islam.

Pebbles are thrown at the walls.

Stoning the Devil

Towards the end of the Hajj, pilgrims travel to Mina to hurl pebbles at three walls, representing Satan. The stoning takes places over three or four days, and at least 49 pebbles must be thrown. After the ritual, men shave their heads and women cut off a lock of hair.

RULES OF IHRAM

*No knots should be tied

*Men must not wear clothing that is stitched together

*Cutting, or plucking, hair is not permitted

*Nails must not be cut

*Women must not wear makeup or perfume

*Quarrelling and bad language are forbidden

*Animals must not be killed

Simple ihram clothing shows equality.

SACRED STATE

Before entering Mecca, pilgrims must enter a state of *ihram*. To do this, the boys and men put on the ihram garments – two white sheets, which they wrap around their body. Women dress in their usual modest clothing, leaving only their face and hands uncovered. This simple clothing is a sign of purity, and shows that all pilgrims, rich or poor, are equal in the eyes of Allah.

FESTIVAL OF SACRIFICE

Hajj ends with *Eid al-Adha*, or the Festival of Sacrifice. This is an important Muslim holiday. It celebrates Ibrahim's willingness to sacrifice his son as an act of obedience to Allah, before Allah intervened at the last second by providing him with a ram to sacrifice instead.

WANT MORE?

The British Museum, Hajj Exhibition ☆ **www.hajjorumrah.co.uk**

ONE GIANT LEAP FOR CANINES

Meet Laika, a Soviet stray who became the first living creature to orbit Earth. No, this is not the plot of a Hollywood movie. It's a true story, and sadly it is not one with a happy ending for its canine star.

Laika was a 3-year-old mongrel.

MOSCOW MUTT

In 1957, Laika was picked up from the streets of Moscow, and taken to a secret Soviet space laboratory for training. Soviet scientists selected strays because they believed they were tough, and could cope with the exteme conditions found in space.

Astrodog training

Laika and two other strays underwent tough training to prepare for spaceflight. In one test, the dogs were placed in centrifuges and forced to endure G-force levels usually experienced at lift-off. After months of training, Laika was chosen as the fittest dog for the mission.

WHAAAAAAA!

Centrifuge

Hot dog

On 3 November 1957, Laika was sent into space aboard *Sputnik II*. Although the nose cone separated cleanly from the capsule, the launch rocket did not. This stopped the spacecraft's heating system from working properly, sending the temperature inside the capsule soaring to a sweltering 40°C (104°F).

Laika was harnessed in the capsule.

THE END

Laika's heart rate more than doubled as she sped into space in her little capsule. Her heart then settled down, and she survived long enough to eat some food. However, after just a few hours in orbit she died from overheating and stress.

Stamp of approval

When news of the tragic mission spread, Laika became a worldwide sensation. Countries including the Soviet Union, Albania, Poland and Mongolia honoured the little dog with postage stamps. There is also a statue of Laika in Star City, where Russian cosmonauts train.

WANT MORE?

Laika proved that it was possible for living creatures to enter space.

Songs from Bollywood movies often become pop hits.

HOORAY FOR BOLLYWOOD!

Movies have been made in Mumbai since 1899 – twelve years before Hollywood filmmakers called 'Action'. At first, the films were silent. Then, in the early 1930s, sound was introduced. The first Indian-made colour film was produced in Mumbai in 1937. Today, Bollywood makes about 1000 films a year.

MAKING A SONG AND DANCE OF IT

Indian moviegoers want a film that delivers *paisa vasool* (value for money), and expect it to last a good three hours. Impressive dance sequences, catchy songs and a happy ending are essential to a film's success.

Haven't we scene this before?

Bollywood produces twice as many films as Hollywood. The films are made so fast that scenes for up to four different films are shot at one time – using the same actors and the same scenery.

NO SNOGGING, PLEASE!

You won't see snogging in Bollywood films. There was plenty before 1947, when Britain ruled India. After independence, the film censor board was created and snogging was given the kiss-off.

Copycats

Film piracy – where people make and sell illegal copies of films – is so common in India that around 80 per cent of Bollywood films are box-office flops, despite being watched by billions of people.

Bollywood is a play on the words Bombay (now Mumbai) and Hollywood.

I'D LIKE TO THANK MY MUM...

Dancer in the dark

The Lady in Black is the most coveted award in Bollywood. The statuette is presented to the winners of the annual Filmfare Awards, the Bollywood equivalent of the Hollywood Oscars.

WANT MORE?

Bollywood information ☆ www.bollywoodtourism.com/bollywood-history

STOCK PILES

In the Middle East, a good carpet is more than just a floor covering or a pretty wall-hanging. It is a financial asset, which increases in value with the passage of time. Valuable carpets are treasured heirlooms, passed down the generations, and occasionally cashed in when times are hard.

Tucked away in vaults below Tehran's bazaar are valuable carpets being stored as investments by shrewd business people.

The wool is handspun.

Rugs are hand-knotted on ground looms.

WEAVER WOMEN

The Qashqai, a semi-nomadic tribe from Iran, are famous for weaving magnificent carpets. Qashqai weavers use wool produced in the mountains and valleys near the Iranian town of Shiraz because the yarn is exceptionally soft and takes a deeper colour than wool from other parts of Iran.

COR, MY FINGERS ACHE!

A weaver's comb keeps the thread straight.

Antique or fake?
Real antique rugs never have green in the background, as it is a holy colour in Islam and shouldn't be walked upon. The most common colours in antique rugs are red and dark blue.

Under the hammer

In 2009, a rare 17th-century carpet woven in Kirman, Iran, fetched £4 million (US$6.2 million) at Christie's Auction House in London. The carpet made 20 times more than expected, setting a world record for the amount paid for such an item.

Bank roll

Some Persian carpets (made in Iran) are so valuable that banks accept them as security against loans. The risk is, of course, that if you don't repay the money as agreed, you will lose an heirloom that may have been in the family for hundreds of years.

SPRING CLEAN

Carpet washers flock to the Cheshmeh-Ali spring, just north of Tehran, to use its pure water to wash the grime out of carpets. Once the carpets are clean they are laid out on the rocky slopes to dry in the sunshine.

I DON'T SEE WHY IT CAN'T GO IN THE WASHING MACHINE!

WANT MORE?

More about Iran ✶ http://kids.nationalgeographic.co.uk/kids/places/find/iran/

THE SAMURAI WAY, OR THE HIGHWAY

From the 12th to 19th centuries, the samurai were the elite warrior class of Japan. They lived and died by a code of conduct called *Bushido*, meaning 'way of the warrior'. Bushido demanded honour, self-discipline and loyalty to one's master. Skilled with swords, horses and bows, the samurai inspired terror on the battlefield, and respect away from it.

MASTERS OF THE SWORD

Samurai training was deeply influenced by the religious ideals of Zen Buddhism. Zen training was used to make a samurai's thought and action as one, so he could strike without thinking – giving his opponent no time to deal a mortal blow.

Steely swords

A samurai's sword was a work of art. It needed to be hard enough to hold a sharp edge, but flexible enough to survive the ferocity of a duel. To achieve this, highly skilled sword-makers folded the molten steel up to 15 times to rid it of all its impurities.

A samurai's sword was sacred, and never left his side.

Ritual suicide

A samurai's honour was so important that he was expected to perform ritual suicide, called *seppuku*, if he disgraced himself in any way, which included being taken prisoner. To do this, he was expected to use his sword to slash open his abdomen, and die a long and painful death.

Seppuku was performed in front of spectators.

Sometimes two contestants in a duel would draw and slash simultaneously, resulting in them both falling dead at the same moment.

COME ON, I CAN HAVE YOU ALL!

Castle of culture

Although they rose to power as fierce soliders, the samurai fancied themselves as cultured people. To prove this, they hosted plays, poetry readings and tea ceremonies in their strongholds, such as Matsumoto Castle in the Japanese Alps.

Alarming armour

The samurai's distinctive armour was made of metal scales bound together into small, overlapping plates, which were joined together by strings. The basic samurai helmet was made from metal plate.

Some helmets were elaborately decorated with horns, devil faces and beards.

WANT MORE?

Learn the way of the warrior ☆ www.youngsamurai.com

CRUMBS, IT'S THE GREAT WALL

Mention of the Great Wall of China evokes an image of a magnificent monument snaking its way across the top of stunning mountains. Unfortunately, nowadays most of the wall is in ruins, and the once-magnificent fortification can be visited only in a few well-protected scenic spots.

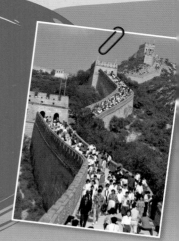

Parts of the wall are over 2000 years old.

SORRY! WE'RE CLOSED!

TOO PRICEY TO POLICE

The Great Wall is around 21,196km (13,170mi) long. It is so vast and expensive to look after that only a few small sections, such as those at the Badaling, Mutianyu and Simatai sites, are protected and well maintained. Other parts are little more than mounds of rubble.

Under siege

The centuries have taken their toll on the wall. Natural disasters, such as storms and earthquakes, have damaged it. Farmers have removed stones to build houses and cattle shelters. Tourists, who smuggle out pieces of the wall as souvenirs, are also responsible for its downfall.

Parts of the wall are crumbling away.

RETURN TO MENDER

In 2003, the maintenance department of the Badaling section of the Great Wall received a carefully wrapped parcel from Canada. Inside was a brick that had been stolen from the wall. The thief, who was guilt-ridden by his crime, had decided to return the brick.

Another brick in the wall

The wall originally took more than a thousand years to build, so you can imagine how long it would take to repair the entire length. However, efforts are being made to restore certain sections. It is a slow and costly process.

TOURISTS TRAPPED

Most Chinese workers get the same annual days off at the beginning of October, which means tourist sites get very busy at this time. The Great Wall can get so crowded that some people only get to see the back of their fellow tourists' heads.

WHERE'S THE TOILET?

WANT MORE?

Mutianyu Great Wall ☆ www.mutianyugreatwall.net

HOLY COW

Cows hold a special position in Hinduism. For Hindus, the cow is *Aghanya*, or 'that which may not be slaughtered', so most Hindus don't eat beef. In the countryside, families have at least one dairy cow for milking, which they treat as a member of the family. In Indian cities, cows roam the streets freely.

283 million
The estimated number of cows in India.

Milk is poured over a statue of a cow as an offering during Maha Shivaratri, an annual festival celebrating Lord Shiva.

QUICK, GET A CLOTH!

FIVE GIFTS OF THE COW

The five products of the sacred cow – milk, curds, ghee butter, urine and dung – are all used in *puja*, or worship, as well as in rites of extreme self-punishment.

Cattle crossing

Delhi's 13 million residents share the streets with about 40,000 cows. This can cause problems, including litter being strewn everywhere as the cows rummage through garbage in search of food. They also present something of a traffic hazard, sometimes causing accidents as vehicles dodge and weave around them.

HMMM! I JUST LOVE DUSTBIN DAY!

Hot cakes

Indian people aren't as grossed out by cow dung as Western people. In fact, they regard it as rather useful. Some people even use their hands to mould the dung into cakes, which are then dried in the sun, and used to fuel cooking stoves.

THEY LOOK BETTER THAN THEY SMELL!

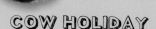

COW HOLIDAY

During the annual Gopashtama festival, female cows are washed and decorated with garlands. Often they are given gifts in the hope that their service to humans will continue.

URBAN COWBOYS

Under pressure to reduce cow populations, Delhi has hired nearly 100 cow-catchers. Their job is to round up the cows and ship them outside the city limits. Some lucky beasts even end up on special reserves.

MOOOVE OVER! WE'RE COMING THROUGH!

WANT MORE?

Facts about Hinduism ✶ www.religionfacts.com/hinduism/things/cow.htm

TWICE THE SPICE

Two spices come from the fruit of the nutmeg tree. Nutmeg is made from the dried-out seed of the fruit. Mace is made from the red membranes, called *aril*, that cover the seed.

Mace

Whole nutmeg

Ground nutmeg

Nutmeg is a seed.

MONEY TREES

Spices from the Moluccas Islands have been enjoyed around the world since ancient times. Until the 18th century, these Indonesian islands were the only place where nutmeg and cinnamon grew. Although the spices were fairly cheap to buy in the first place, they passed through the hands of so many traders, that by the time they reached Europe they were an expensive luxury.

TRADE SECRET

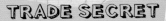

Until the 16th century, Arab merchants shipped the spices to Venice. To protect their monopoly, they made up wild stories about where the spices came from. Many of these tales involved Sinbad (right), a greedy spice trader who got into many scrapes.

Cut out the middle men
In the early 16th century, the Portuguese found sea routes to the Moluccas. The Europeans then conquered the islands, building fortifications and army settlements, so that they could take total control of the valuable spice trade.

I'M OKAY. I'VE GOT NUTMEG UP MY NOSE.

DE REEDE VAN BANDA.

Dutch trading ships

Fill your beak

In the 16th and 17th centuries, the price of nutmeg soared in Europe. This is because people believed that it protected them against bubonic plague. Plague doctors wore beaked masks filled with nutmeg and flowers, thinking the mixture would purify the air.

Dutch dominance

At the end of the 16th century, Dutch traders seized the Moluccas from the Portuguese. Like the Portuguese, they banned the export of live seeds and trees to ensure the spices couldn't be grown anywhere else. They even soaked dead seeds in lime juice to make sure they wouldn't grow.

GONE FISHING!

Until 1863, the Dutch banned the native people of the Moluccas from growing anything other than spices. Today, fish and other sea products are the main source of income. The profits in spice are just not what they used to be!

THERE'S MORE MONEY IN FISH NOWADAYS!

BACKERS ANDT

=

In the 16th century, a small sack of nutmeg could buy you a grand house in London.

WANT MORE?

NO ONE'S SAID A THING ABOUT MY NEW PARKA!

FUR OR BRRRR!

Although many Siberian people wear modern, man-made fibres, those out in the forest and tundra wear more traditional animal skins that are far warmer. Reindeer fur is the fur of choice, as each hollow hair shaft is filled with air, which gives added insulation.

The Nenet people layer themselves in skins and fur to herd their reindeer across Siberia's icy wastelands.

Meat and no veg

Summers are short, so there isn't much time to grow fruit and vegetables. This means that people eat a lot of fish, reindeer and horsemeat. Although this doesn't sound very healthy, people get vitamins and minerals from milk and other dairy products. And they don't just milk cows. They also milk horses, sheep, goats and camels.

CHILLY CHALLENGES

The far north of Siberia is one of the coldest places on Earth. Winter temperatures can drop to a toe-tingling −60°C (−76°F). Surprisingly, people do actually live and make a living here. But how do they cope with everyday life in such extraordinary conditions?

People even light fires beneath cars to keep the diesel in the fuel tanks from freezing.

Taking the plunge

Some Siberian people think that taking a dip in freezing water is good for the health. Fans of icy plunges claim they rarely get colds and reckon they'll never suffer pneumonia.

PASS THE SOAP! QUICK!

Burying the dead

The ground in Siberia is so frozen that it takes up to three days to dig a grave. First, hot coals are piled onto the site. A couple of hours later they are scraped off, and the ground is dug. The coals are pushed back into the hole, and the ground dug again. This goes on until the grave is 2m (6.5ft) deep.

CENTRAL HEATING

In Russian Siberia, the term 'central heating' has extra meaning. In some towns, centrally controlled heating plants provide the entire community with electricity and steam heat. The pipes that carry the steam to houses can't be buried in the frozen earth, so they are laid above ground.

Coffins sometimes rise to the surface after years of freezing and defrosting.

WANT MORE?

Russia ☆ http://kids.nationalgeographic.co.uk/kids/places/find/russia/

Sun block

When Krakatau erupted it spewed pumice, ash and rock 80km (50mi) into the sky. Average global temperatures fell by as much as 1.2°C (2.16°F), as clouds of sulphur dioxide and ash covered the sun.

Pumice

Hot pumice up to 20cm (7in) in diameter rained down.

BLOWING ITS TOP

Krakatau is one of the most famous volcanoes in the world. It lies in the Sunda Strait, between the islands of Java and Sumatra. When it last erupted in 1883, it blasted its way into history. Thousands of people were killed, and towns were razed to the ground. After the eruption, temperatures around the world fell and weather patterns were chaotic for years.

MMMM! IT DOES SEEM A BIT CLOUDY TODAY... NOT TO WORRY!

FOOLHARDY FESTIVALS?

Ash and smoke rose from Krakatau for two months before it erupted. But rather than evacuating the island, the locals held festivals instead. The party mood ended on 26 August with the first of a series of large explosions. By the next day, two-thirds of the island had been blown into the sea. Today, there is an annual celebration of the event.

Washed away
If the ear-splitting noise, choking ash and red-hot rocks weren't enough, the eruption also created enormous tsunami waves up to 40m (131ft) high. Together the volcano and waves destroyed 165 villages and towns and killed more than 36,000 people.

Hot ash covered nearby islands.

Huge waves hit Java and Sumatra.

BIG BANGS

With an explosive force 13,000 times the power of an atomic bomb, the noise produced by the eruptions burst the eardrums of sailors in the Sunda Strait. The same sounds were heard over 3000km (1864mi) away in Perth in Western Australia, and over 7000km (4350mi) away in Sri Lanka.

37

Aerial displays
The eruption changed the world's skies for days, months and even years. The dust caused darkness up to 400km (250mi) away. Close to the volcano it remained dark for three days. There were exotic colours in the sky, halos around the sun and moon, and spectacular orange sunsets and sunrises as far away as New York, USA!

WANT MORE?

Witness reports ☆ http://teacher.scholastic.com/activities/wwatch/volcanoes/witnesses.htm

MEALS ON WHEELS

Each dabbawalla picks up around 35 tiffin carriers, and then takes them to the train station by trolley or bike. Here, they are handed over to another dabbawalla, who takes them to an unloading station. The containers are sorted into destinations, rather like the mail, and then delivered to the correct addresses.

MMMM! ME THINKS MR SINGH HAS GOT DAHL AGAIN.

LEGENDS IN A LUNCHTIME

Every working day, dabbawallas ferry containers of freshly prepared food from the homes of 200,000 Mumbai city workers to their workplaces in time for lunch. The 5000-strong army of delivery men battle the chaos of the Indian city's streets with such extraordinary efficiency that huge multinational companies hold them up as a good example of how to organize a business.

Stacks of flavour
Three to four stacked boxes snap together to form an Indian lunchbox, known as a tiffin carrier. Each storey contains a different type of food, such as rice, vegetables, or slices of pickle and salad.

Commuter hell

Getting through the chaos of Mumbai is no mean feat. Trains are very overcrowded, and the streets are full of dangerous traffic, including the odd cow. And when the monsoon season hits, the dabbawallas have no choice but to wade through filthy water to hit their delivery deadlines.

On average, each tiffin container changes hands four times, and travels 60-70km (37-43mi) on its journey to its hungry owner.

Each dabbawalla has the same number of clients and is paid the same amount.

THE CODE

Tiffin carriers have a 99.999999 per cent chance of arriving at the right destination. The dabbawallas know where each tiffin should be delivered and returned to by the code on the top of the container.

As many dabbawallas can't read, the containers are colour-coded.

Fussy beefeaters

The Mumbai food delivery system is more than 120 years old. It began in 1890, during British rule in India, and was for British army officers, who wanted British food rather than the local spicy delights.

WANT MORE?

Indian culture ☆ www.culturalindia.net

TRAINED KILLERS

In central Asia and the deserts of Mongolia, eagle masters
have been hunting with golden eagles for around 6000 years.
Being an eagle master is a life-long profession, and the skill
is often passed down from father to son. Some hunters
compete in hunting festivals, pitching their eagles
against those of other hunters.

BIG BIRD

The golden eagle
weighs up to 12kg
(25lb), and has a 2.4m
(7.8ft) wingspan. It uses
its powerful talons to lift
animals weighing up to 5kg
(11lb). Their usual prey is hare,
rabbit and large birds, but they
have also been known to take
foxes, young sheep and goats.

2.4M (7.8FT)

A young eagle master
with his bird

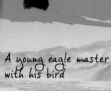

PLEASE COME
BACK...
IF NOT,
TWEET ME.

Bird-knapped

Eagles are taken from the nest as
chicks. It can take up to a year of
daily handling before the eagle
understands and recognizes its
master's calls. The master must go
for long periods without sleep
while he tends to the young bird.

Hunting takes place in winter.

> There are three things a real man should have: a fast horse, a hound and a golden eagle.
>
> *Kazakh proverb*

Hunting festival
At competitions, the eagles are judged on how well they can catch and kill their prey. The hunting contests end with a ceremony to honour the winning trainer.

LOOKS LIKE I'M ABOUT TO BECOME A HAT!

The hood must be comfortable.

Winners of the Golden Eagle Hunting Festival

HOODWINKED

The master makes the eagle wear a hood over its eyes for weeks on end during the training period. This helps the eagle to develop a relationship of trust and dependence with the master. The hoods are later used to keep the birds calm when they are on their masters' arms.

WANT MORE?

Golden eagles ★ www.avmv20.dsl.pipex.com

FEARSOME GODS

In ancient Asia, people believed in many different gods and goddesses. Most of the gods were kind. But there were some that could do terrible things if they were made angry. To keep the gods happy, people prayed to them and left them offerings. The only gods that nobody was safe from were the Gods of Death. When they came calling, there was nothing anybody could do.

Head severed during the battle

Tongue hangs from her mouth

DON'T MAKE ME CROSS!

BLOOD ON HER FOUR HANDS

The Hindu Mother Goddess Kali can be kind, or dark and violent. During one battle, she killed so many people that Lord Shiva threw himself under her feet to stop her. Kali was so surprised her tongue shot out of her mouth.

Girdle made of arms

String of heads for a necklace

Bowl to collect the falling blood

Burly bouncers

Evil spirits don't mess with the Door Gods Qin Shubao and Yuchi Jingde, so their images are painted on doors across China. They started out as generals in the Tang Dynasty army, but were elevated to Door Gods when they scared off a demon that was pestering the Emperor.

Battery-charged bellybutton biter

The Japanese Shinto god Raijin doesn't go anywhere without the ring of drums he uses to make thunder. He also carries a fully charged lightning maker. According to legend, Raijin enjoys eating children's bellybuttons.

I'LL JUDGE YOU AFTER YOU DIE!

GOD OF DEATH

Yama, the Hindu God of Death, rules Kalichi, the ancient Indian underworld. He rides a buffalo, and holds a mace in one hand.

When a person dies, Yama decides if they go to Kalichi, paradise or another existence on Earth. Evil souls are tortured in Kalichi. They may be boiled in oil, ripped apart, or thrown into rivers to be gnawed by water demons.

During thunderstorms, some Japanese parents tell their children to hide their bellybuttons so Raijin can't devour them.

WANT MORE?

Chinese gods ✴ www.historyforkids.org/learn/china/religion/gods.htm

MUD, SWEAT AND EARS

An ear of rice might take just three months to grow, but it takes a lot of hard work. Heavy farm equipment is rarely used. The land has to be ploughed by hand, or with a rotavator, or using a water buffalo. Then every seedling has to be plugged into the muddy pools.

I WISH I WORKED AT THE BANK!

RICE TO MEET YOU

'Have you eaten your rice today?' is a common greeting in China, Bangladesh and Thailand. And in China, instead of wishing you 'Happy New Year' people say, 'May your rice never burn!'

Lakshmi

Food of the gods

In India, rice is associated with Lakshmi, the Hindu Goddess of Wealth. In Japan, it is said that the Sun Godde: Amatereshu-Omi-Kami grew rice in the fields of heaven. Ir Thailand, offerings are made Mae Posop, the Rice Goddess to ensure a good harvest.

RICE OF LIFE

Rice is the staple diet of billions of Asians. Many people eat it for breakfast, lunch and dinner. About 95 per cent of the world's rice is produced and eaten in Asia. Thailand ships out the most – about five million tonnes a year.

In much of Asia, poor people spend half to three-quarters of their incomes on rice!

NOW WHERE WAS THAT BASMATI?

IN THE BANK

The Rice Gene Bank in the Philippines holds over 117,000 samples of rice. Researchers use them to develop new rice varieties and farming techniques that they hope will improve its quality and yield.

195kg (430lb)

3kg (6.6lb)

The average person in Myanmar eats 195kg (430lb) of rice each year. The average European eats 3kg (6.6lb) per year.

Gifts of the grain
Rice is incredibly versatile. Rice straw is made into rope, paper, bricks, clothing, shoes and toys, and twisted into fuel sticks.

Crackers

Rice grains

Wine

Grain is cooked as rice, made into wine, crackers and cereals, brewed into beer, and ground into cosmetics. Rice bran is put in food to add fibre, and made into oil for cosmetics. Hulls are used as packing material and burned as fuel. Ash from hulls is used to clean discoloured teeth.

WANT MORE?

Rice facts ✶ www.historyforkids.org/learn/food/rice.htm

BIG IN JAPAN!

DOES MY HAIR LOOK OKAY?

Sumo wrestling is Japan's national sport, and the wrestlers are adored by millions. Sumo dates back 2000 years, and is steeped in the traditions of the Shinto religion. To begin with it wasn't a spectator sport, it was performed to satisfy the gods. Today, a sumo wrestler, who is known as a *rikishi*, still has to live by a strict set of traditional rules. In return he earns fame and fortune.

TOP KNOTCH!

As soon as a sumo wrestler becomes an apprentice, he grows his hair long so that he can wear it in a topknot. These are styled by specially trained hairdressers. There are two types of knot – the *chonmage* and the *oichomage*.

An apprentice sweeps the ring.

Before a match, wrestlers purify the ring by throwing salt onto it.

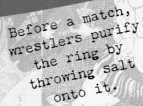

Stable boys

Wrestlers live in training 'stables' together with a stable master, referees, ushers and hairdressers. Wrestlers are divided into a hierarchy based on performance. Apprentices help look after the higher-ranked rikishi.

WAKEY, WAKEY!

Wrestlers train for three hours a day, starting at 5am. Next is a sparring session, when a lower-ranked wrestler stays in the ring until he is defeated by another rikishi. This is one way that apprentice wrestlers can work their way up the ranks.

What a pushover!

Two rikishi begin a bout by crouching down in a straw ring, with their fists on the ground. Then they charge! The aim is to push the opponent out of the ring or force him onto the floor. A rikishi loses the match if any part of his body lands outside the ring, or if any body part other than the soles of his feet touches the ground.

Most fights last just seconds.

Nothing to declare

Rikishi actually spend most of their time performing Shinto ceremonies. The first one on tournament day is the *dohyo-iri*, or ring ceremony. During this, rikishi parade around in highly embroidered aprons, called *kesho-mawashi*, before lifting them to show that they have no hidden weapons.

Ring ceremony

EASY NOW, BOYS!

WEIGHT WATCHERS

Sumo wrestlers work hard to gain weight. They scoff two huge meals a day – eating about four times as much as the average adult. Meals consist of a hearty stew called *chanko-nabe*. After gorging, they lie down for a nap to help them put on more weight!

WANT MORE?

SKY BURIAL

People living in the high mountains of Tibet don't bury or burn their dead. They cut them up and feed them to vultures in a religious ceremony known as a sky burial. This isn't as callous as it might sound, as Tibetan people believe that vultures are like angels that will carry the person's soul into the heavens.

Spirit of the sky
In a land where the ground is too rocky to dig graves, and wood is too scarce to perform cremations, the vulture is revered as a 'holy eagle', performing a sacred job.

Incense

LONG GONE

After a person dies, they are cleaned and wrapped in white cloth, before being carried by chanting monks to a 'charnel' ground. Once there, incense is burnt while a *rogyapa* prepares the body for the vultures. He begins his gruesome task by cutting up the body, and removing the flesh from the bone with an axe or flaying knife.

Bone breaker
The sweet scent of incense, mingled with the smells from the body, attracts hungry vultures. While the vultures tear into the flesh, the rogyapa begins to smash the bones.

A rogyapa

TO BE HONEST, I'M MORE THAN A BIT PECKISH MYSELF!

BONE MEAL

The powdered bones are mixed with barley flour and water to form a paste, which is thrown to the waiting birds. And in this final gesture, the body of the deceased returns to nature.

WANT MORE?

Sky burial facts ✫ www.travelchinaguide.com/cityguides/tibet/sky-buria.htm

A LIVING TRADITION

In Borneo, up to 20 families can live in one longhouse. The Iban tribe find many advantages to this way of life. For instance, there are always other kids to play with. And, if you want to learn something, you simply watch the adults in the communal area. Chores, food and belongings can be shared. Above all, the Iban believe in helping and having fun together.

WHO WANTS TO DO MY HAIR TODAY?

FAMILY QUARTERS

Families do have their own private rooms. There is also a decked area for each household, and a piece of farmland somewhere nearby.

Gathering place
The house is divided along its length by a partition. On one side of this are the family rooms, and on the other is a long hall. The hall, which is a type of communal gallery, is where all the work is done.

All mod cons
Most longhouses have running water, electricity and even the Internet.

Carving out a reputation
Wooden sculptures, created by the men, are used to decorate the longhouse. From an early age, Iban boys learn how to carve by watching other men. Boys and men are very proud of their sculptures. It is normal for young men to carve bamboo containers as gifts to impress the ladies.

AREN'T I A PRETTY BOY!

WOMEN'S WORK

Iban women are very proud of their weaving skills. Talented weavers spend most of their time in the longhouse inventing new patterns and designs. The Iban decorate their houses with them or sell them to tourists.

Until about 50 years ago, the Iban were headhunters. They often kept skulls as mementoes. These gruesome trophies are still on display in some longhouses.

WANT MORE?

Learn more ☆ www.malaysiasite.nl/ibaneng.htm

ANYTHING YOU CAN DO...

A strip of land 4km (2.5mi) wide divides North Korea from South Korea. This buffer zone was created as part of the Korean Armistice Agreement in 1953. Although the zone is known as the Demilitarized Zone (DMZ), it is the most heavily guarded border in the world.

The Panmunjeon Flagpole in the North

North Korean soldiers watch every move in the south, while the soldiers in the south do exactly the same.

HA-HA! OUR FLAGPOLE IS TALLER THAN YOURS!

FLAGPOLE WAR

In the 1980s, the South Korean government built a 98.4m-tall flagpole (323ft) to fly the national flag in Daeseong-dong. The North Koreans responded by building a flagpole 160m (525ft) high in Kijong-dong. On the top is a 30m-long North Korean flag (98ft).

Standing tall

Only South Korean soldiers over 1.7m (5ft 6in) tall are selected to patrol the DMZ. It's believed their height (which is 5cm (2in) above the national average) makes them look intimidating. They must also have a black belt in martial arts.

NORTH KOREA

1 million
soldiers guard the Demilitarized Zone.

HE'S LOOKING AT US AGAIN ISN'T HE!

248km
(154mi)
The length of the buffer zone between North and South Korea.

SOUTH KOREA

REGULATION JEANS

Tourists visiting the South Korean side of the DMZ are not allowed to wear ripped clothing. The South believes the North Koreans would broadcast photos of the tourists to convince their people that the Western world is so poor that people have to wear threadbare clothes.

Dodgy coal mines
Since 1974, the South has discovered four tunnels crossing beneath the DMZ. North Korea claims the tunnels were dug for coal mining. No coal has been found in the tunnels, but some of the walls have been painted black to look like coal.

WANT MORE?

South Korea ✶ http://travel.nationalgeographic.co.uk/travel/countries/south-korea-facts

Before the game
The carcass is soaked in water for 24 hours before play. Sometimes sand is packed inside to make it heavier.

BET THAT PACKS A PUNCH!

DANGEROUS HORSEPLAY

Afghanistan's national game, buzkashi, is one of the roughest games in the world. Played on horseback, the aim of the game is to keep control of a headless goat's carcass. During the game, players routinely suffer cuts and bruises and break limbs.

COME ON, HIT HIM WITH IT.

Catch me if you can
The game has been played in Afghanistan since the 13th century. Back then, men on horseback would often steal goats or cattle. The herdsmen came up with tactics for protecting their livestock, and the game of buzkashi was born.

Huge crowds flock to watch buzkashi. Games often bring a village to a standstill. Sometimes spectators get so excited that fights break out!

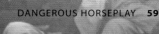

HOW DO YOU PLAY?

The carcass is placed in a chalked-out circle. At a set signal, all the horsemen race to grab the carcass and gallop away with it. The winning rider is the one who carries the carcass into the winning circle. Other riders try to stop this by snatching it however they can. The game can also be played between two teams.

DON'T GET SADDLED WITH A BAD HORSE!

It is impossible to win a buzkashi competition without a specially trained horse. The horses know to stop if their rider is thrown off, and they also know they must gallop off at speed if their rider manages to grab the carcass.

DID THAT SEEM FAIR TO YOU?

Rules, what rules?

Competitors are not allowed to secure the carcass to their saddle, or hit an opponent's hands to get hold of the carcass. Other than that, it is generally a free for all. Punching in the face and kicking are allowed.

WANT MORE?

Buzkashi ★ www.afghan-web.com/sports/buzkashi.html

IN DIRE STRAITS

For centuries, the Strait of Malacca has been plagued by pirates who steal cargoes, kidnap crews and even hijack whole ships. With about 50,000 ships a year passing through the narrow strait, targets are easy to spot. Fortunately, since the countries in the region have joined forces to fight piracy, there has been less trouble.

40% of the world's trade passes through the Strait of Malacca.

Westports Malaysia is one of many huge ports on the Strait.

RICH PICKINGS

The Strait of Malacca is one of the most important shipping lanes in the world. It connects the Indian Ocean and the Pacific Ocean, and carries oil from the Persian Gulf to China and other Asian countries.

South China Sea

Strait of Malacca

MALAYSIA

INDONESIA

SINGAPORE

The 800km (497mi) trade route is a seascape of tropical islands and secret coves, providing plenty of hideaways for the pirates.

Raiders and hijackers
Piracy attacks range from small-scale robberies by desperate men armed with guns, to highly organized hijackings of giant vessels by teams of professionals.

Captured pirates

I'M ONLY TRYING TO EARN A LIVING!

STAMPING OUT PIRACY

By 2004, piracy was affecting local trade. The three countries in the region – Malaysia, Indonesia and Singapore – agreed to join forces to fight the problem. Since then, piracy has declined and many pirates have been put behind bars.

Anti-piracy police

AHOY YOU SALTY SEA DOGS!

WANT MORE?

Pirates ☆ www.thewayofthepirates.com/history-of-piracy/modern-piracy.php

THE WORD ON PAPER

Chinese people have been using paper since the 2nd century AD. To begin with they used it to make decorations, such as lanterns. People even made clothes out of it. And by the 3rd century AD, writing on paper instead of bamboo or wood was common.

INGENIOUS INVENTIONS

The ancient Chinese invented an amazing number of everyday things, including silk cloth, toilet paper and the wheelbarrow. Among their most important inventions were paper, printing, the compass and gunpowder – all things which have helped shape the history of the world.

Paper was dried on frames.

THIS NEW PAPER STUFF WILL CHANGE THE WORLD.

Silk making was a closely guarded secret.

Paper-making process

Early paper was made from a boiled mixture of mulberry tree bark, hemp and linens. This pulp was pounded into paste and stirred with water. Then a wooden frame with a mesh of reed was dunked into the mixture, shaken and hung up to dry into paper sheets.

The handle of the spoon, which was made from magnetic lodestone, always pointed south.

An early spoon-shaped compass

Getting the point

The magnetic compass was first invented in China around 221–206 BC. To begin with it was used to ensure homes were built facing north, which the Chinese believed would keep the buildings in harmony with nature. Later, the compass was used for navigation at sea.

Wooden printing block

The bronze plate was decorated with markings for north, south, east and west, and star constellations.

BIG BANG

In the 8th century AD Chinese alchemists (who experimented with all sorts of potions) mixed sulphur, charcoal and saltpeter to make gunpowder. At first it was used to produce smoke and fireworks, but before long it was used to make weapons.

Moveable type

THE TYPE THAT MOVES

The Chinese were the first people to use printing. In the beginning, a whole page of text was carved onto a single block of wood, which could only be used once. Then, in around 1045 BC, Bi Sheng invented the first known moveable type printing. Single words were carved on separate clay blocks, which could be used again and again.

Gunpowder was used in fireworks.

WANT MORE?

Ancient China ☆ www.historyforkids.org/learn/china/

BLACK GOLD

Before 1937, the Saudi royal family weren't amazingly rich. The country's economy was based on agriculture, and the major exports were things like dates, camels, sheep and horses. The king's only real income came from taxes paid by pilgrims visiting Mecca. But that all changed when oil was discovered by US geologists. The vast reserves of oil totally transformed the kingdom's economy. Now the royal household is enormously rich, and many of its members lead lavish lifestyles.

King Fahd's palace in Marbella was modelled on the White House in Washington DC.

FAMILY BENEFITS

About 40 per cent of the Saudi government's income goes to the 40,000 members of the royal family. Senior royals get much more cash than minor royals. Having more children can also boost earnings, and lump sums are handed out for building palaces.

King Fahd on a riyal note

Saudi Arabia is the world's largest producer and exporter of oil.

WE'VE COME A LONG WAY IN A FEW DECADES!

Costa de lotta money
From the 1970s, King Fahd, Saudi ruler from 1982 to 2005, spent every summer in Marbella, on the Costa del Sol, Spain. On his last visit, the king arrived with a fleet of jumbo jets. By the time he left seven weeks later, he is said to have spent about £60 million (US$91 million).

The Marbella palace is called Mar-mar.

The current Saudi ruler, King Abdullah Al Saud, owns more than 1000 horses, including hundreds of purebred Arab horses.

Playground of the rich
Prince Abdul Aziz, favourite son of the last king, has his own private theme park in Riyadh. Costing an eye-watering £3 billion (US$4.5 billion), it includes a palace and a scale model of old Mecca.

Plenty of time
From January 2004 to April 2005, the Saudi ambassador to Britain, Prince Mohammed bin Nawwaf, bought 43 watches at a cost of £350,000 (US$530,000). Just one of them set him back £23,000 (US$38,000).

SUPER YACHT
The *Prince Abdulaziz* yacht is owned by the Saudi royal family. At 147m (482ft) long, it is the fourth largest luxury yacht in the world and is reported to have cost £123 million (US$186 million). It has a swimming pool, jacuzzi, helipad, a fully equipped hospital, a mosque and cinema.

WHERE'S THE JACUZZI?

Members of the Saudi royal family own 18 of the top 100 super yachts in the world.

WANT MORE?

Super yacht facts ★ www.superyachts.com/motor-yacht-3536/index.htm

WHOOO! I HAVE MAGICAL POWERS!

Basket case
A ninja could easily hide his face beneath the basket of a komuso monk.

A DYING ART

Until quite recently, ninjas (secret assassins with skills in spying and sabotage) were active in Japan. Their secretive lives were very different to those of the honourable samurai warriors. Due to their secretive nature, not a lot is known about the ninjas. There is, however, a wealth of folktales, which usually give the ninja superhuman powers.

DEVIL IN DISGUISE

While the movies always show ninjas clad in black clothing, they were never that easy to identify. They were usually disguised as ordinary people, such as priests, farmers or monks. This allowed them to operate in plain sight without detection.

SUPERMEN

Some of the superhuman abilities given to the ninjas include flight, invisibility, control over animals and the elements, as well as the ability to walk on water. The last one may be partially true, with the ninjas using circular wooden boards on their feet to float and bamboo paddles for propulsion.

TACTICS

Ninjas used sneaky tactics to avoid discovery. When slipping into a castle, a ninja might distract guards by starting a fire elsewhere. Another strategy was to throw duckweed onto the surface of water to hide his movement underneath.

SABOTAGE

Fire was the main form of sabotage practised by the ninjas. Castles and enemy camps were the main targets.

SUPER SPIES

Spying was the chief role of the ninjas. Using their skills in disguise, deceit and stealth, they gathered information in enemy terrain and relayed it back to the people who hired them. Ninjas were often paid by samurai to spy on their enemies, and do their dirty work.

I MUST DO SOME SHOPPING LATER.

Grappling hook and rope

Tools of the trade
Ninjas used a large variety of tools and weaponry, some of which were specialized. This included tools used to sneak into castles, such as grappling hooks, ropes and collapsible ladders.

WANT MORE?

Explore Japan ☆ http://web-japan.org/kidsweb/explore/history/q4.html

Nothing can live in the salty water, which is why it is called the Dead Sea.

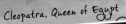
Cleopatra, Queen of Egypt

BY ROYAL APPOINTMENT

The Dead Sea is a salt lake bordered by Israel and Jordan. According to legend, Queen Cleopatra built the first-ever health spa along its shores more than 2000 years ago. Today, people still visit the lake to enjoy the health benefits of its waters, air and even its mud.

Salt crystal formations

THE ONLY WAY IS UP

Once a river flows into the Dead Sea, the water has nowhere else to go but up. It is evaporated by the heat of the Sun, leaving salt behind. The high concentrations of salt in the remaining water make it very buoyant, so anyone can float in the Dead Sea without effort.

> "...very bitter and salty water in which no fish can live and where neither man nor animal can sink."
>
> *Greek philosopher*
> *Aristotle (384–322 BC)*

Hot bath
Thermo-mineral springs are dotted along the Dead Sea shore. The hot water contains lot of minerals that are thought to be good for treating joint problems.

Dead Sea water	Ocean water
29% salt	4% salt
71% water	96% water

MUD BATH
Visitors slather the thick black mud found along the shore all over their bodies, and then wait for it to dry before washing it off in the sea. The mud contains 26 different types of minerals that are believed to be good for the skin.

DO YOU THINK IT WILL GET RID OF MY SPOTS?

The highs of the lows
Lying more than 400m (1312ft) below sea level, the Dead Sea coast has the highest atmospheric pressure recorded on Earth. The air here, which has up to 8 per cent more oxygen per cubic metre (35cu ft) than air at sea level, is said to ease the breathing of people suffering from lung diseases.

WANT MORE?

GREAT TRAIN RIDE

The Trans-Siberian Railway is the longest railway in the world, linking Moscow with the port of Vladivostok, 9297km (5776mi) away. After its seven-night, eight-day journey, passengers will have travelled almost halfway across the world, seeing two continents and 800 train stations.

Standard cabins are super cosy

+3 = Greenwich Mean Time + 3 hours

Moscow
Yaroslavl
Kirov
Perm +5
Ekaterinburg
Tyumen
Omsk +6
Novosibirsk
Krasnoyarsk +7
Tayshet
Irkutsk +8
Ulan-Ude
Chita
Skovrodino +9
Belogorsk
Khabarovsk +10
Vladivostok
+3 +4

TIME TRAVELLING

The route passes through eight different time zones, so depending on which direction a passenger is travelling in, they will either be going back in time or forwards in time.

Moscow time
All the trains run on Moscow time. The times displayed on clocks at stations outside Moscow's time zone bear no relation to the departure time of the train. This can be very confusing!

DON'T GO FAR. WE'LL BE LEAVING SOON.

Time keeper
People can pop off the train to stretch their legs when it stops in stations. The length of the time spent at each stop varies. Carriage conductors keep a close eye on wandering passengers, letting them know when the train is about to leave.

THINGS TO TAKE WITH YOU

☆ A pocket-knife for slicing up bread and vegetables which can be bought from sellers on the platforms

☆ A torch for reading when others want to sleep

☆ A flask for hot water

☆ Tea, coffee, instant noodles or soup

☆ A large mug

☆ Snacks

Teatime
A large urn, known as a *samovar*, is kept at the end of each carriage. It is always full of boiling water for making tea.

WANT MORE?

Life on the train ☆ www.waytorussia.net/TransSiberian/Life.html

SAY IT WITH A MAUSOLEUM

The Taj Mahal is one of the most famous sites in India. The love story behind it has been melting the hearts of people since the 17th century. The tale is that of a Mughal emperor who was so grief-stricken by the death of his wife that he built a magnificent crypt for her body to rest <u>in</u>. The marble monument is so dazzling that it is regarded as one of the most splendid buildings in the world.

BUILDING EMPIRE

Born in 1592, Shah Jahan was emperor of the Mughal Empire in South Asia from 1628 to 1658. He is considered one of the greatest Mughal leaders. He was responsible for building many great structures, including the Taj Mahal at Agra.

The emperor and his wife are buried beneath the white dome.

YES, I'VE TOLD YOU A MILLION TIMES, YOU ARE THE FAIREST OF THEM ALL!

Labour of love

Building the monument took a lot of time and effort. Architects from all over the world designed it. White marble for the façade was transported more than 300km (186mi) from Makrana to the site. And it took 22 years for 20,000 labourers to complete.

Jewels of the palace

When Shah Jahan became emperor, he gave the title Mumtaz Mahal, meaning 'Jewel of the Palace', to his third wife. Mirroring this honour, Shah Jahan had the walls of the entire monument (inside and out) inlaid with precious gems.

OFF WITH THEIR HANDS!

According to one gruesome legend, Shah Jahan had the hands of the Taj Mahal's architects and workers chopped off after it was completed to ensure they never built another of its kind.

> The sight of this mansion creates sorrowing sighs;
> And the sun and the moon shed tears from their eyes.
> In this world this edifice has been made;
> To display thereby the creator's glory.
>
> *Emperor Shah Jahan*

Together again

When he died, Shah Jahan was buried inside the Taj Mahal alongside his beloved Mumtaz Mahal. The emperor actually had three other wives – we can only imagine what they thought of the funeral arrangements!

WANT MORE?

Taj Mahal facts ☆ http://tajmahal.gov.in

I HAVEN'T GOT TIME FOR MATES.

Gamers can socialize in gaming arcades.

LIVING IN A FANTASY WORLD

Fantasy worlds become almost real to gaming addicts. Mobile devices mean that they can spend most of their day taking part in role-playing games, slaying dragons and rescuing damsels in distress. However, in the real world many young South Korean gamers have few friends.

WIRED NATION

South Korea is one of the most tech-savvy nations in the world. Around 98 per cent of households have broadband and many children can play computer games before they can read and write. In fact, Korean children are exposed to so much technology that many are becoming addicted to it.

There are now South Korean fairytales in which children fall prey to Internet addiction.

WOW, I DIDN'T REALISE I HAD TWO SISTERS!

Getting the family back online

Internet addiction is a serious problem. Addicts become moody, tired, and often can't concentrate at school. Special camps, where families learn to do things together in the great outdoors, have been set up to help them. The activities may not seem as exciting as computer games, but they do drag addicts away from the Internet.

Computer curfew

Thanks to a law nicknamed the 'Cinderella Law', South Korea now pulls the plug on young gamers between midnight and 6am. Their computers don't suddenly turn into pumpkins – instead the players' access is blocked. It does not affect mobile devices, however, so many addicts still manage to get their 'fix'.

WARNING SIGNS OF ADDICTION

- Constantly worrying about the game or computer when away from it
- Fibbing about the amount of time spent on the Internet
- Growing distant from friends and family who had previously been close
- Becoming defensive about the amount of time spent on the Internet
- Spending a silly amount of money on computer-related things
- Losing track of time

WANT MORE?

Internet addiction ☆ www.netaddiction.com

HARD HAT REQUIRED

Dubai's World Trade Centre, Dubai's first skyscraper, was competed in 1979. At the time, it was the tallest building in the Middle East. Twenty years later, building work in the city went into overdrive and more and more high structures were added to the skyline. Just 30 years after the construction of the first skyscraper, Dubai became home to the tallest building in the world.

Desert islands

The ambitious architecture is not limited to skyscrapers. Dubai's builders have created islands in the sea. The World is a group of 300 man-made islands, built to represent the world's landmasses. Made mainly from dredged sand, only one of the islands has actually been built on.

Burj Khalifa

I SAID I WANTED REMOTE BUT THIS IS RIDICULOUS!

RECORD BREAKER

Burj Khalifa, the tallest man-made structure in the world, rises 163 floors to a height of 829.8m (2722 ft).

It takes 36 workers up to four months to clean the exterior of the Burj Khalifa.

I'LL GO AND GET SOME MORE WATER!

Burj Al Arab

THE HIGH LIFE

The world-famous Burj Al Arab hotel stands on an island of reclaimed land. It took three years to reclaim the land and less than three years to construct the building itself. It was designed to resemble the sails of an Arab sailing ship. The hotel, one of the most luxurious in the world, is 321m (1053ft) tall.

Self-service
The interior of the Burj Al Arab is decorated lavishly. Although it is officially a five-star hotel, the owners have awarded themselves seven stars!

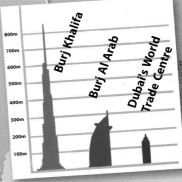

Burj Khalifa
Burj Al Arab
Dubai's World Trade Centre

800m
700m
600m
500m
400m
300m
200m
100m

The sky's the limit
Burj Khalifa is 4.5 times the height of Dubai's first ever skyscraper. It took just 30 years to achieve such heights. Who knows how tall the buildings will be in another 30 years?!

A brave new world
The Palm Islands in Dubai are a group of three artifical islands, designed in the shape of palm trees. On the islands are luxurious hotels, and the homes of some of the richest people in the world.

WANT MORE?

The Palm Islands ☆ http://thepalmdubai.com

SILK ROAD

6500km
(4040mi)
The total length of all the silk trade routes.

Rome

Istanbul

Damascus

Suez

Baghdad

Basra

Tashkent

Peking

Thai

Canton

Ma

Aden

Bombay

TRAVELLING SALESMEN

More than 2000 years ago, merchants from the East and West began to establish a network of trade routes that linked Asia with Europe. The routes became known as the Silk Road, because of the Chinese silk trade that ran along it. The Silk Road brought together different cultures which exchanged ideas, technologies and religions.

IMPORTS AND EXPORTS

Goods moved in both directions along the routes. Sheep, wheat and bronze came from the West. Paper, silk, iron and steel were among the goods that came from the East.

In the 1320s, the Black Death made its way from China to Europe along the Silk Road.

FOUR-LEGGED HGV

The merchants travelled on foot, while camels carried the goods. Camels were not speedy animals but they were hardy. They could carry more than 100kg (220lb) over long distances without needing water. The travelling groups of traders and camels were called caravans.

SHE'S TOUGH AND DOESN'T DRINK MUCH.

Life on the road
It was tough-going along the routes. Brutal winds whipped up sandstorms, and the mountains were difficult to pass. There was one nice section – a string of fertile oases known as the Gansu Corridor. However, traders had to cross the mountains or the desert to reach it.

The Great Wall

Khiva, Uzbekistan

The Wild East
Bandits took advantage of the terrain to rob caravans, forcing the merchants to employ costly guards. Sections of the Great Wall in China were built along the northern side of the Gansu Corridor to stop bandits from harming trade.

Lasting legacy
Over centuries, the Silk Road developed its own societies which built temples and cities, such as Khiva in Uzbekistan. Their customs, laws and technologies were influenced by the different cultures of the people that travelled the route.

WANT MORE?

The Silk Road ✶ http://china.mrdonn.org/silkroad.html

THE HIGH LIFE

Sherpas are a tough group of people who live among the high peaks of the Himalayas in Nepal. There are no paved roads so they have to travel everywhere on foot. They carry anything they need on their backs, or on the backs of their faithful yaks.

Hillary and Norgay

Wage hike

When Edmund Hillary and his Sherpa guide, Tenzing Norgay, conquered Mount Everest (the world's tallest mountain) in 1953, it sparked a tourism boom. Today, people flock to Nepal to go trekking, and many employ a Sherpa guide. Some Sherpa guides can earn five times the average Nepalese salary.

SUPER SHERPA

Sherpas are elite mountaineers, and regularly serve as guides on climbing expeditions. Apa Sherpa has climbed to the top of Mount Everest a record-breaking 21 times. It took him four attempts to reach the summit for the first time, which he did on 10 May 1990.

Sherpas are devout Buddhists, who respect all living things, and revere the mountains.

Apa Sherpa

Sherpa villagers gather yak dung from the trails and dry it into patties, which they use to fuel their stoves.

WHERE DID WE PACK THE TIN OPENER?

YAK!

WESTERN WAYS

While many Sherpa communities have no running water or electricity, larger villages do have some mod cons. Satellite dishes beam in foreign TV channels, and people keep in touch with the world via the Internet.

Living off the land

About 80 per cent of the 70,000 Sherpas living in Nepal are poor farmers who grow most of their own food. The staple crop is potato. These were first introduced to the region in the 1800s from the English gardens of Kathmandu.

> Sherpas can carry loads heavier than themselves.

> Yaks can carry up to 100kg (220lb).

All-terrain vehicle

Yaks, which cope well with the rock-strewn mountain trails, do the job of trucks and tractors. These hard-working animals are not just beasts of burden. They also provide the Sherpas with wool for clothing, leather for shoes, dung for fuel and fertilizer, and milk, butter and cheese.

Everything, including the sink

When a Sherpa family wants to build a new house everything has to be physically carried up the mountain. It is not unusual to see a porter lugging a loo uphill, or even a rooftop solar heating tank. Luckily Sherpas are famous for their strength.

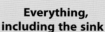

WANT MORE?

More about Nepal ☆ www.welcomenepal.com

WHY LIVE HERE?

The river floodwater is full of silt, which is rich in nutrients, making the land fertile. Rice grows particularly well in this kind of soil.

High and dry
Some families build their homes on stilts, which lift the houses well above the floodwater. Other people live in houses raised up on mounds made of earth.

THAT WATER WASN'T THERE WHEN I FELL ASLEEP.

Half of the land in Bangladesh is covered in water – rivers, lakes and ponds.

THE LOWS

Flooding is incredibly common in Bangladesh. This is because it lies at the mouth of three major rivers, and a quarter of the land is just 1m (3.3ft) below sea level. Every year the rivers burst their banks when monsoon rains hit. And if that isn't enough, Bangladesh also experiences many tropical cyclones, which cause the low-lying land to be flooded by coastal waters.

10 million
The number of people living in areas at risk of flooding.

Cyclone shelter
Built of solid concrete and raised off the ground by about 7m (23ft), cyclone shelters are the best place to be when a storm hits. They may not be pretty, but a single building can save the lives of thousands of people.

SURF 'N' TURF

When livestock is your livelihood, you don't want it floating off or drowning, so farmers build raised platforms to keep their animals safe and dry.

Satellite image of cyclone

MUM, THE COWS ARE UP HERE.

FLOOD WARNING

When a cyclone begins to form in the Bay of Bengal, the weather department sends out warnings to 50,000 volunteers based in villages. The volunteers raise flags in public places to warn people of the coming storm. They may also use megaphones and sirens to spread the word

Effects of flooding
- Thousands killed
- Homes destroyed, and people made homeless
- Spread of diseases, such as cholera
- Crops destroyed and animals killed
- Shortage of drinking water and food

WANT MORE?

MONGOL MOB

Genghis Khan was one of the greatest military leaders of all time. Originally called Temujin, he united many different nomadic tribes in Mongolia around 1205. He was so successful that the Mongols renamed him Genghis Khan, or the Great King. Genghis Khan led a powerful army, which conquered nearly all of continental Asia, the Middle East and parts of Eastern Europe.

Genghis Khan

22%
of the Earth's land was ruled by the Mongol Empire at its height.

Horse trading
The soldiers were expert riders, who began training at 15. Each soldier was given three or four horses. By changing them regularly, the cavalry were able to travel at high speed for days on end without tiring out the animals.

THIS SPEAR IS HEAVY!

HEY, TRIGGER, YOU LOOK READY FOR A BREAK.

MIND GAMES

The Mongols spread terror to towns and cities even before they arrived. First they offered a town the chance to surrender and pay tribute. If the offer was refused, the Mongols would invade and destroy the settlement. They allowed a few people to flee so that they would spread fear to neighbouring settlements by reporting what had happened.

GET OFF MY LAND!

Siege machines

Large catapults were an important part of Mongol warfare, especially when attacking fortified cities. The armies travelled with mostly Chinese and Persian engineers, who built the catapults from wood and other materials found at the site.

WEAPON OF CHOICE

Mongol soldiers were deadly with the bow and arrow. Its shape and size allowed it to be fired in any direction from horseback.

WE WILL DEFEAT YOU ALL!

WANT MORE?

Genghis Khan ☆ www.history.com/topics/genghis-khan/

ECCENTRIC, ME?

Since the break-up of the Soviet Union
in 1991, Central Asia has become
a hotspot for vain despots.
The most eccentric of all was probably
Saparmurat Niyazov, self-proclaimed
President for Life of Turkmenistan.
He died in 2006, but his successor
has proved almost as outlandish.

ME!

VANITY PAIR

Niyazov littered the Turkmen
capital, Ashgabat, with countless
statues of himself. In the city's main
square, a 12m-high (39ft) rotating
gold statue of him sat on top
of the Arch of Neutrality.

ME!

ME!

Every bit
of Turkmen
currency had
a picture
of Niyazov
on it.

What's in a name
Niyazov changed
his name to
Turkmenbashi, which
means 'father of all
Turkmen'. He renamed
the country's main port
city after himself, and
renamed the months
after his mother.

I'M IN CHARGE NOW

When Kurbanguly Berdymukhamedov took over from Niyazov, he changed back the names of the months, and took down some of his predecessor's statues. Then he began making his presence felt everywhere. Massive images of him feature heavily at national events, leaving everyone in no doubt about who is in charge of the country.

ME!

ME!

I'M A DENTIST, A SPORTSMAN, AND A GREAT PRESIDENT!

ME!

Berdymukhamedov seems set on creating his own legend as a man of action. He even managed to win the country's first motor race!

NUMBER ONE!

Berdymukhamedov loves to break world records. Here are some he has had a go at:

- ☆ World's biggest enclosed Ferris wheel (95m/312ft tall)
- ☆ Biggest handmade rug in the world (301sq m/987sq ft) *
- ☆ World's tallest flagpole (133m/436ft tall) *
- ☆ World's largest star-shaped structure (211m/692ft tall)

1st

* *Record no longer stands*

WANT MORE?

Their special day
President Berdymukhamedov has ordered brides and grooms to plant trees and visit the capital city's main monuments on their wedding day. The lucky couples get to see such romantic sites as the Earthquake Memorial, the Monument to the Constitution, the Monument to Independence and a Second World War memorial.

Before becoming a politician, President Berdymukhamedov was a dentist!

SCOOTING THROUGH TRAFFIC

In cities packed with people, it is easier and quicker to get through traffic on a scooter than in a car. Finding a parking space is also much less hassle.

HURRY UP, I'M GOING TO BE LATE FOR WORK.

DAD, WHEN CAN I HAVE A SCOOTER OF MY OWN?

I'M SURE WE'RE MISSING SOMEBODY!

SCOOTING AROUND THE CITY

The roads in southern Asian cities are teeming with motor scooters. They are particularly popular in India, Vietnam and China because they are manufactured there. They are owned by so many people because they are far cheaper to buy and run than cars. They also have many other advantages over other vehicles.

Family vehicle
For some, a scooter is the family vehicle. It is amazing how many family members can fit on one. It might look incredibly dangerous to us, but for many it is the only way to travel.

3 million scooters are sold in India each year.

SHOW-OFFS

Young, more well-off Chinese people have lost their taste for the humble bicycle, and now favour scooters instead. Some owners have their bikes customized with artworks or other added features to make them stand out from the crowd.

BUSINESS BIKE

With a bit of imagination, it is amazing what a scooter can be used for. Some are custom-made into all-weather taxis, while others have open trailers added for carrying goods.

WANT MORE?

See a busy Asian road ☆ www.youtube.com/watch?v=oetF3UTIwbc/

LIVING LIKE A MONK

Boys and girls can be sent to Tibetan Buddhist monasteries when they are just six years old. When they enter the monastry, these youngsters are called 'novices'. For many novices, joining a monastery is a way of getting an education or finding peace – but not all the novices end up becoming monks and nuns.

> WAKEY, WAKEY.
> TIME FOR
> PRAYER AND
> MEDITATION.

NO REST FOR THE GOOD

After only five hours sleep, novices are woken by the sound of a gong or bell. The day is divided into activities, including study, duty (perhaps sweeping or laundry) and ritual. After the evening meal and prayers, novices are tested on what they learned that day. They go to bed around midnight.

Monk making clothes

Earning a crust

There are services and duties a monk or nun can perform to earn money for food. They can sit with the bereaved or dead in the local community. Or, as long as it doesn't disrupt their duties, teaching and learning, they can make and sell things.

The novices are allowed two cups of tea each day.

Jasmine tea

I KNOW THIS ONE OFF BY HEART.

Feeding the mind
The novices' food and any extra tea they drink is supplied by their families or sponsors. Jasmine tea is a luxury, which monks or nuns have to buy for themselves.

School of thought
Schools are an important part of monastic life, and study can last around 18 years. The novices are taught Tibetan language, grammar, literature, religious texts and prayers. As they progress, the novices are taught longer, more complicated texts.

I WISH THEY'D ALL SHUT UP. I CAN'T THINK.

HEY, I THINK I WON THAT ARGUMENT.

NOISY NOVICES
Buddhist monasteries aren't quiet places. The grounds are filled with the noise of monks chanting different religious texts, and debating with each other. Debating helps the novices to understand Buddhism.

WANT MORE?

Buddhism is the fourth biggest religion in the world.

WHY HERE?

During its long history, Jerusalem has been destroyed twice, besieged more than 20 times, attacked over 50 times, and captured and recaptured more than 40 times. It has no ports or natural resources and the water is of very poor quality. So why are people so interested in the place?

Christian church

Most Christians believe the ground on which the Church of the Holy Sepulchre stands is Golgotha, also known as the Hill of Calvary. This is where the Bible says Jesus of Nazareth was crucified. The church is also said to contain the place where Jesus was buried – the sepulchre – which sits just below the building's domed roof.

The sepulchre

THE SIMPLE ANSWER

Jerusalem is home to sites that are hugely important to the world's three main religions – Christianity, Islamism and Judaism.

Church of the Holy Sepulchre – a place that has been a centre of Christian pilgrimage since the 4th century

Western Wall – the one remaining wall of a Jewish temple destroyed in 70 AD. It is the most important Jewish site

Dome of the Rock – the third most important site in Islam

Temple Mount (site of the Dome of the Rock) – a religious site for thousands of years, used by all religous groups

WALL OF PRAYER

Jews from around the world gather at the Western Wall to pray. People often write notes to God and place them between the ancient stones.

Notes left for God

Al-Buraq

ISLAMIC SHRINE

The Dome of the Rock contains the rock from which the Prophet Muhammad is said to have ascended to heaven after a journey from Mecca to Jerusalem on the winged steed Al-Buraq.

WANT MORE?

Jerusalem ☆ http://sacredsites.com/middle_east/israel/jerusalem_facts.html

INDEX

NOT-FOR-PARENTS

ASIA
EVERYTHING YOU EVER WANTED TO KNOW

1st Edition
Published September 2013

WELDONOWEN

Conceived by Weldon Owen in partnership with Lonely Planet
Produced by Weldon Owen Limited
An imprint of Red Lemon Press Limited
Northburgh House,
10 Northburgh Street
London, EC1V 0AT, UK
© 2013 Weldon Owen Limited

Project managed and commissioned by Dynamo Ltd
Project manager Alison Gadsby
Project editor Gaby Goldsack-Simmonds
Designer Richard Jewitt
Picture researcher Sarah Ross
Indexer Marie Lorimer

Published by
Lonely Planet Publications Pty Ltd ABN 36 005 607 983
90 Maribyrnong St, Footscray, Victoria 3011, Australia

ISBN 978-1-74321-912-6

Printed and bound in China by 1010 Printing Int Ltd
9 8 7 6 5 4 3 2 1

www.redlemonpress.com

Red Lemon Press Limited is part of
the Bonnier Publishing Group
www.bonnierpublishing.com

Credits and acknowledgments
KEY – tl top left, tc top centre, tr top right, cl centre left, c centre,
cr centre right, bl bottom left, bc bottom centre, br bottom right.

All images © Shutterstock except:
14cl, 14bl, 14cr, 15cr, 40bl, 52bl, 54bl, 59c, 68bl, 69bl, 70tr, 70bl, 89br, 93bl
Alamy; 8tl, 8tc, 8br, 9tl, 9cl, 9cr, 9br, 10tl, 11tl, 11cr, 12bl, 13tl, 13br, 16bc,
17bl, 18cl, 18cr, 19tr, 19br, 20bl, 20br, 21cl, 23tl, 25tl, 25cl, 26tl, 27br, 28tr,
28cr, 29br, 33c, 33b, 36cr, 37tr, 37br, 37tl, 37bl, 37br, 43tl, 43bl, 44cr, 45t,
45cr, 46bl, 47cr, 49tl, 50tl, 50bl, 51cr, 52cr, 53tr, 53br, 55cl, 56tr, 56cl, 54bl,
55cl, 58tl, 58br, 59tl, 60tl, 60b, 61tl, 61tr, 61br, 62bl, 63c, 67bl, 72tl, 73cr, 77tl,
77cl, 77bl, 78cr, 80tr, 82cr, 83cl, 83tr, 84bl, 85cl, 88c, 88cr, 92bl **Corbis**;
8tr, 13bl, 16tl, 17cl, 18bl, 19tl, 21tl, 28bl, 34tl, 36bl, 43cr, 44bl, 47tl, 54c, 64bc,
66cr, 68tl, 69tr, 75tl, 76cl, 78tl, 79cr, 82tr, 82cl, 85tr, 86bl, 87tr, 87c, 88tt, 89cl,
89c, 90tr, 90cr **Getty Images**; 64tl, 64cl, 65b, 71tr, 71cl, 87cr, 90bl **Rex
Features.**
Cover illustrations by **Chris Corr**
All illustrations and maps © 2013 Weldon Owen Limited

...AND RELAX!

LONELY PLANET OFFICES

Australia Head Office
Locked Bag 1, Footscray, Victoria 3011
Phone 03 8379 8000   Fax 03 8379 8111

USA
150 Linden St, Oakland, CA 94607
Phone 510 250 6400 Toll free 800 275 8555 Fax 510 893 8572

UK
Media Centre, 201 Wood Lane, London W12 7TQ
Phone 020 8433 1333 Fax 020 8702 0112

lonelyplanet.com/contact

MIX
Paper from
responsible sources
FSC™ C021741